MW00888201

THIS BOOK BELONGS TO